Ultimate Game of Life

Mystical Reflections

Ultimate Game of Life
Mystical Reflections

Ashok Saighal

(Foreword by Dr Karan Singh)

Manas Publications
(We Convert Fighters into Writers)
New Delhi-110002 (INDIA)

MANAS PUBLICATIONS
(Publishers, Library Suppliers, Importers & Exporters)
4402/5-A, Ansari Road (Opp. HDFC Bank)
Darya Ganj, New Delhi-110 002 (India)
Off. ✆ 23260783, 23265523, Res. ✆ 23842660
Fax: 011-23272766
E-mail: manaspublications@vsnl.com
manaspublications@yahoo.com
manaspublications@gmail.com

ISBN 978-81-7049-417-1
₹ 300/-

Designed by
Manas Publications

Printed in India at
RK Offsets, Delhi
and published by Mrs Suman Lata for Manas Publications,
4402/5-A, Ansari Road (Opp. HDFC Bank),
Darya Ganj, New Delhi-110 002 (INDIA)

Dr. Karan Singh
MEMBER OF PARLIAMENT
(RAJYA SABHA)

3, NYAYA MARG
CHANAKYAPURI
NEW DELHI - 110 021

15 July 2009

Foreword

Though it is hard to divine the nature of reality from the untold wisdom of the mythic traditions, the author in these refreshingly original verses takes a modern reader on a rollercoaster ride into the underlying meaning of life, the universe and reality.

Ashok Saighal writes verses that flow from the wisdom tradition of Osho and calibrates them for the "SMS-generation" by writing verse that they can jive to. The profundity in the addictive 'lyrics' seems to be ideally suited for the short-attention spans that many of us have developed in the so called communications age.

All the verses in ***The Ultimate Game of Life*** explore the 'game of life' through vastly different lenses such as astrology, gender, master, spiritualism, technology and create a vibrant discourse that can serve as a guide to understanding (and navigating) our existence, if we can incorporate his central lesson to seek and then harness the silence that underlies our life and the universe.

Karan Singh

Tel. : 2611-1744, 2611-5291 Fax : 2687-3171
E-mail : karansingh@karansingh.com

Doing is the being of being; Joy is the seeing of seeing
The one who is seeing is the same who is being
The one who is being is the same who is seeing
Once been there is nothing left to see;
And once seen there is nothing left to be.
Now who is doing this being and seeing?
It is the master fool; the spark of all sparks;
The joy of all hearts; the torture of all minds
It alone exists, all belongs to it. It is the
only sense. Rest is all nonsense.

Tolerate your presence.
Drown your ego in your presence.
At the bottom, you will not be absent
Nor will you be present.
Nor will there be the presence of the
sense of being absent.
You will hear a strange laughter
You will be laughing without laughing
It will never stop; because there will be no
time there to stop it.
It will not get bound; Space will not be there to bind it.
Only laughter will remain.
Spiritualist is always laughing.
Egoist is always learning how to laugh.
Stop learning. Just laugh.
Stop fearing. Just laugh.

Love loves.

Compassion creates.

Passion destroys.

A child does not care. God does not care.

All caretakers are devils in disguise.

Stop passion. Stop compassion. Stop loving.

Become care-less; and free yourself from the need to care.

Caring is not a need.

It has to be care-less caring.

It cannot work otherwise.

Renounce the preacher.

Play with a child and realize the truth.

I saw many beautiful things.
In so many different places.
Suddenly, she came
And I knew what beauty was.
The mystic monk offered me the best of his honey.
He had put his heart into it.
God, it was so sweet.
Suddenly; from nowhere she came,
offered me her lips.
And I knew what sweetness was
And now I am her slave.
Slave to her beauty, slave to her sweetness.
I look up and she becomes more beautiful and more sweet.
I have stopped looking at her. It is too beautiful.
I am happy looking down. I am her slave
She calls me her best slave.
I dare not look up.

Thousands of years it took
for the yogi to learn his yoga
Proudly he played his yoga to the master
The master remained silent
The yogi showed off his Lotus position
The master was silent
Achtanga was preformed by the yogi
The master was still silent
Frustrated, the yogi sat down in silence
It was very difficult. He was so used to performing.
He begged the master to teach him the yoga of Silence.
The master did not move;
but a voice was heard from his heart.
It said "yogi unlearn your learning" and enjoy
the beauty of silence. Why not listen to that
voice now and give up the need to learn?
Learning never ends. Silence remains forever.

The Master brings you down
The fool takes you up
The master is the fool
I am Real
The universe is a game
I am the game
Technology is a sin
Realise it.
It is okay to sin.
God forgives.
There is no God
It is only an idea.
Depends how you see it.
That which is, is not.
This is mad. Stop the madness.
How? No one knows. Only all knows.
One is all.

Who was that fool who said love is strong
It is the weakest emotion I know of.
The intense burning desire to belong
is what I must learn to get rid of.
But how? I love this pain and want of it more
Till the breath of life reaches its final shore.
Through the passage of time, through the river of life
The pain slices through me like a butcher's knife.
Enough! No more, like a babe, I yell.
But the damn pain is what I want like hell.
This is not a complaint my love, nor a fight.
Stupid me always gets the wrong end of the bite.
So hurt me, move on and find your new start.
But let me at least love the pain of my broken heart.

The lord of paradise began to play his music.

The mistress of heaven began her dance.

So beautiful was the music that she was hypnotised; so beautiful was the dance that he was hypnotised.

He did not want to stop his music because the dance should not stop; she did not want to stop to dance because the music should not stop.

In this total rapport, who should make love and to whom? Protections are not necessary; a child does not happen; the universe does not happen. Music and dance becomes eternal; absorption becomes eternal; celebration becomes eternal.

Give that paradise to your woman and win heaven from her.

Awareness plays the music through the sounds of silence; consciousness does the dance through waves of illusions. All this is that.

The master of hell has a problem.

He has no one left to drag into his net of darkness and excitement.

He gives up and splits into two.

One half of him becomes music; and the other half joins the dance.

The story, the storyteller, the music and the dance become one and remain one without hellish fears of distortion of its oneness.

All impositions are impressions

All expositions are expressions

What you are is an impression

What you appear to be is an expression

There is an impeccable identity between what

You are and what you appear to be

You impress me and I express you. Vice-versa.

Crossfire between expressions produces a round

When coloured with ego, it is a live round; very harmful.

Without the ego, it is a blank-round; very harmless.

Seen from the Source, where impressions and expressions are mutually negated, it is neither a live round nor a blank round; but a very joyful merry-go-round. Only a child has that perception.

So become a child and have fun.

My spirit fools me.
My mind cheats me.
My heart confuses me.
Where then is my truth?
I have stopped looking.
In emptiness I hear a sound
In the void I see an image
And I know I am being fooled
Who is that 'who,' who is fooling me?
It must be cleverer than me
Why don't I accept it? I will tomorrow.
Tomorrow never comes.

Freedom to choose is not freedom.

It is bondage.

Your choice binds you.

Your preferences limit you.

In order to be free, you have to become foolish.

A fool trusts.

He knows that all ends well.

He has no doubt.

Only the fool has the privilege of randomness.

Teachers want to remove your foolishness.

The master encourages the fool within you.

The fool has given up his brain.

The brain is there. The fool does not use it.

The teachers boast of their brain-power.

The master shows his heart.

Feminity is the illusion.

The other is always the feminine.

The other is in the brain.

It has no *locus standi.* I am the other.

The syndrome ends.

How many candles will you light to overcome darkness?

Why not choose the bright zone? Everything is obvious in brightness.

There is no excitement there; only joy.

Everything is hidden in darkness.

Very exciting.

There is no joy there; only misery.

Darkness is the mother of brightness.

Brightness is the father of darkness.

Both are in the mind.

"Light-less-ness" is the reality.

It is not bright; nor is it dark.

It just is.

It underlies all dark and bright unrealities.

Why are we struggling to prefer brightness or darkness? Both are unreal.

The struggle is also unreal. Body, mind and brain are also unreal.

So is the soul. Unreal.

My head fulfills my heart
my heart inspires my head
why then do I not mind my own business?
Who taught me to put my head in other
people's hearts? My greed and my naked desire.
Desire is always naked. If it is pure,
it has no shame and needs no body.
If it is impure, it puts on a body.
The more impure it is, the more beautiful is the body.
A pure desire frees itself from
the obligation of a body.
Misery ends.
And yet, all of us are body-focused.
Focused on becoming strong.
Joy has no body.
It has no mind.
It needs no focus.
It is always present, here, now.

He is spiritual; she is not
He contemplates; she gossips
He is natural; she uses a lot of make-up
He goes after things; she wants the things to come to her.
He gives her the sperm; she gives him birth
Such is the nature of He and She
Let him be He; let her be She
And enjoy the love and the hate between He and She.
One day, He and She will dissolve in the sea
of spirituality and god will rise from the same sea
to create a new He and a new She.
When will this non-sense end?

The Flower dies; the tree survives
The tree dies; the seed survives
The seed dies; the earth survives
The earth dies; the space survives
Space dies; time survives
Time dies; nothing survives
Nothing dies; the flower appears again.

The yogi realizes God.

The egoist keeps on looking for God.

The yogi tames his animal nature by sitting over it.

The egoist pretends to be tame by wearing a necktie.

The yogi experiences strength by discarding the gun and overcoming his sexuality.

The egoist wants a super gun and a banana dick to feel powerful.

This is all male talk. Where is the story of a woman?

A woman is beautiful. Very beautiful.

Her job is to inspire the universe through her beauty.

A yogi appreciates her beauty; encourages her to become more beautiful.

She calls him a master.

An egoist fucks her beauty.

She calls him a lover.

When she gets tired of him, she calls him a beast, a disgusting beast.

Ask a woman.

She knows the truth of her story.

Want to enjoy a game? Watch a child playing and learn how to play.

Want to win a game? Go find a coach.

You may win but it no longer will be the joy of playing.

It will be the stress or excitement of competition.

Want to enjoy yoga? Find a yogi and do 'yog' with him. Want to learn yoga? Find a yoga teacher.

The teacher will teach you yoga but destroy your natural balance; thereby defeating the very purpose of yoga.

Yoga has only one purpose – to enjoy your natural balance.

A game has only one purpose – to enjoy your natural talent.

Out with the coach and the teacher.

In with a child and a yogi.

A yogi is an adult who has neither forgotten the child with-in; nor the unborn potential with-in.

He holds on to the unborn while playing the role of the born through the eyes of a child.

A great fucker wins a bronze medal
A great thinker wins a silver medal
A great lover wins a gold medal
A child does not care
Ignoring this simple truth, the ego keeps
on looking for medals. Surrender yourself
to the child with-in and enjoy careless
winning or careless losing. Joy lies in that state.

Feminine intrigue is spicier than male on-slaught.

A child's mischief has more spontaneous uplift than feminine intrigue.

I leave it to you to decide who wins the gold medal.

If your answer is on-slaught than you are a sick-woman, if it is intrigue then you are a sick man; if it is mischief then you are a child yourself beyond adult sickness; and ready for entry into paradise.

If you still insist on seriousness, you shall re-incarnate into a very painful life with painful systems and it would become increasingly difficult to be mischievous, which is a prelude for entry into paradise.

Investing in time is a waste of time.
Invest in space. Not cyber space. That is dumb.
The real space is in your heart.
It gives birth to time. Be on it; play
with it and enjoy bliss forever. Do not excite
yourself there. If you do, you will have to enter it.
Once in, you will be thrown back as time.
The cycle of time must end.
Karma too must end. Joy is the key.
Excitement is ignorance. Joy is bliss.
Joy cannot be born. Joy is an unborn child.
It is aware of bliss. It has no ignorance.
It is faultless. It is here. It is not in now.
Now is a mid-point between past and present.
The real now is here; in your heart.
Stop searching it.

Disappointment is the mother of frustration,
Fear is the mother of anger
Unfulfillment is the mother of pity
Where have all the fathers gone?
I guess they are busy chasing women.
Stop impressing women. If you do,
You will be born as an expression.
Expressions feed on impressions.
Ego feeds on expressions.
Why can't you enjoy women?
Joy cannot be born.
Joy has a fullness. It has a ripeness.
It is sweet to all hearts.
Find that joy within yourself and share it.
Impressionism and expressionism will stop to exist.
Joy will be everywhere.
So, what are we waiting for?
Someone to impress us?

"Doing" as the being of "Being" is unified, unilateral, absolute, free from duality and therefore painless.

"Doing" as separate from "being" with this line of thinking that "I am doing it", misses the point. It creates a separate universe which is diversified, bi-lateral, relative, trapped by subject and object relationships, full of pain and pleasure and bound by laws of "Space-time". Ego is the knot between being and doing.

The never-ending bliss of pure "Being" is powered by the uncaused sound-less sound of the mantra "Aum".

Cherish this mantra "Aum" as your true nature which is beyond "Being" and "Doing", beyond "Real" and "Unreal", unreachable through effort.

So what is this struggle all about?

While on the surface; enjoy the surface. Some spiritual seeker will frustrate you.

"You have to find your depth", he will say. Do not listen.

When you are deep, enjoy your depth.

"You have to find your rock-bottom" is the comment some seeker will make.

Do not listen.

When you are at the rock-bottom, enjoy it.

Here too, some intellectualist will interfere.

"You have to find your top" will be commented. Do not listen.

Enjoy your level.

Do not reach out. Float on your level.

Lose awareness of all other levels.

Lose awareness of your level too.

Be aware of floating.

Soon, you will lose yourself. Only float will remain.

Floating and floating, forever and forever.

You will be the float of the spirit, the joy of the spirit, the sparkle of the spirit.

You alone will be.

All will be of you, from you and for you.

You will be least bothered.

You will have no care.

And no spiritual seeker can reach you there to remind you that you are careless.

The relationship which the moon has to the

earth is same as the ego has to your heart.

The relationship which the sun has to the earth

is same as your "I-go" has to your brain.

Moon is the mistress of space.

The sun is the master of time. Space is visible; time is invisible.

Visualize the moon and have fun; romantic or lunatic.

Do not visualize the sun. if you do,

your vision will get destroyed. Moon

has the master key of cubicology. The sun opens

up squarology.

It all looks like geometry or is it ego-matrix? Seen from below it is

all geometry.

Seen from above it is ego-matrix.

Or is it the other-way around? Why do things

always end up in confusion.

I guess we have to find the master key of confusion. Confucius had it.

Search him again.

Mental re-cycling is a retarded function.
At your end-point, express gratitude and
move on to the higher ladder.
There is only one problem.
The ladder never ends.
Cleverness misses the point.
Wisdom grabs it.
Do not reject yourself.
Reject the ladder.
Once out of it, you will have a big laugh.
The ladder was only a refraction in your vision.
Stop seeing. Only be. Seeing is not being.
Seeing is with-in being. This is very confusing
Don't blame me. Blame the words.
The wise one neither writes, nor talks.
I wonder if he sees.
Once been, there is nothing left to see.
Where did I hear that?

Creating phenomenon endlessly or explaining it endlessly is a sick mental futility.

Its temporary gratification falls far short of the intense and painful complications this intrusion creates in the original scheme of things.

Instead, hold steadfastly to your being.

Creation would then be seen as an unnecessary extension; purely mental.

Its only purpose is to question its reality or validity to the point of exhaustion.

There, we give up and return to our original state of un-alloyed bliss.

So why not be original right now and enjoy bliss endlessly? This is not what we are being taught.

Out with the teacher; in with the Guru.

"I am this" is religion.

"I am that" is ego.

"I am" is existence.

Existence feeds on the fight between religion and ego. One day, "I am this" will get tired of its fight with "I am that".

Existence too, will get tired by its "I am-ness".

All three will drop down to rock-bottom.

There in the state of "non-existence," "I am it" will be

revealed to me as my true nature.

I will be alone there; I will have no need to impress anybody; I will have no

desires; I will have no doubt; no questions no answers.

I will be a never ending spark; full of joy and happiness.

Oh! You teachers of this world don't teach me anything,

let me be.

Let me realize my non-existence which is the purpose of living.

Act as a man

Re-act as a woman

Respond as a child

Play like a man

Win like a woman

Have fun like a child

Take pain as a man

Heal it as a woman

Cry it out as a child

Lead like a man

Be-led like a woman

Follow like a child

It appears that the child has the most natural response. So

why not be child-like and be natural.

That what is natural

is spiritual. Nature is feminine.

So the concept of God has to be a woman, who powers the man, but favours the child.

There is no birth, no death, no past no future.

There is no soul, no ego.

There is no present. There is only "IS". "Is" is not an experience of the present.

It is simply being

"is", and realizing that is-ness is the nature of "is" just

like wetness is the nature of water.

Thinking, meditation, yoga, concentration, prayers are all ineffective techniques which can actually fatten the ego.

Contemplation is the mother of all techniques.

It is an effortless method to trace your ego back to its source. So

if yoga & meditation and prayers do not improve your

contemplation and do not help you in going inwards, stop wasting time, money and energy on it.

I belong to her. She belongs to him.

She and he are sweet-hearts.

I am their fun. I am being used.

I don't like this.

So I start again.

I belong to her.

She belongs to him.

Him is rooted in me.

Me is the duality in I.

I shoots up from the self.

Even this is too much.

I give up my cleverness and start again.

It becomes clearer.

I am the self.

There is no He or She or Me or I.

There is only the self which can mirror itself but cannot see itself through I, Me, He or She.

How frustrating? But truth is bitter.

Sweetness is the illusion caused by sweet-hearts.

Does that mean that the self is bitter? How can the self know? It has no senses.

It is forever drunk.

I am the all-mighty spirit.

My name is woman.

I am always sixteen.

I never die. You cannot look at me directly.

I am too beautiful for your eyes. Instead, be a man, if you can and win a shape and form from me. But,

in the end I will destroy you and take you back into my virgin womb where you shall rest in bliss till the end of time, till another fool attacks my virginity and recreates you.

Choice is yours.

Enjoy me from with-in or try to possess me.

You will lose.

I said to you, I am the all-mighty spirit.

I am always behind you. I am also your master.

My name is woman, the divine mother.

There is no holy father.

He never was.

I alone am.

I am the holiest of all forms.

My name is Siva-Lingam.

It has the colour of gold.

It is full of joy.

It is immune to excitement.

It has no testicles.

It never sits down.

Millions of shes have tried to excite it.

It retains its joy.

They dance around it and experience the joy of the dance.

On the fourteenth day of the glorious dance the joy is so great that the lingam sucks them in.

Once in, the women realize that their beauty itself had powered the dick.

There they rest in bliss, unafraid. A perfect state of golden silence is reached where women with silver wings dance the cosmic dance.

Paradise is experienced. Duality

syndrome fades away from vision.

Experience stops.

Bliss happens. Sixteen is realized.

Hello! I am the source.

I power the spirit.

I am always sparkling.

My name is innocence.

You can call me Ganesha.

Millions of Hes and Shes have tried to fool me into birth. I remain unborn.

I am foolproof.

I have a dream.

My dream is to be sixteen.

My dream inspires me,

I inspire the dream.

But my dream cannot fool me.

I am fool-proof.

Do not try to catch me.

I am beyond all beyonds.

I am absolute, the ultimate existence; forever existing; forever blissful.

Foolishly, I call myself

Ganesha, to give joy to your spirit.

The man wants his power. The woman wants her beauty.

The child wants his fun. Try having fun.

While you are having fun, the thought about power and beauty cannot arise.

It arises when fun stops. God is not a woman.

God is not a man. God is not a child. That makes God powerless, beauty-less and fun-less. Do I want to reach that God? Good heavens, no. He lives for her. She lives for life. Life feeds the magnet of the ego. Ego powers existence. Need to dominate existence is ignorance. Darkness of ignorance is removed by the never-ending light of the same boring God who never does anything, never gets bankrupt and hence can always be depended upon to re-start the business of life from its humble beginnings.

The guidelines are on your hands.

The silence is within your heart.

Be in contact with that silence and read out your lines. That is what the melodrama of life is all about.

Your silence has a sound.

Those who heard it call it Aum.

But then the intellect raises a question.

How can silence have a sound? Empty vessels do make a noise.

So what stops the empty heart from making a sound. It does.

Those in tune with the sound of that silence therefore declared the universe to be causeless.

Reflect on this today.

Women have arrived.

Kali has happened. The writing is clear on the wall. The day of the bull is over.

Womanagement will be taught by the universities.

Management will become obsolete.

The stock-exchanges shall rewrite their language.

Cats & bitches will replace the bulls and the bears.

Male heart will feel very sad.

Not forever though. Eventually, the bitch will lose her heat.

Her heart will melt.

She will re-appear as a very milky cow to breast-feed the fallen down man.

A new dick will rise on the horizon to re-start the wheel of the bulls and the bears.

When will this circus stop? Or does the show have to go on forever?

In every loop there is a hole. It is called a loop-hole.

Enter it with full trust and free yourself.

Do not fix the

hole. If you do, the over-head loom will create a more complex hole.

The teachers will use their brain power to help you fix the hole.

That will trap you deeper into your

karma cycle. The guru will guide you through the hole and free you from your karma. Renounce the teacher and

embrace the guru. The guru and a child have similar qualities.

The pain of the crucified Jesus, or the forced laughter of Budha is inferior in quality to the joy of self. Joy is your natural state. It gives birth to itself effortlessly and does not put on the make-up of a concept. All other births are products of excitement or lust or frustration or anger requiring a subject and an object. The glorious, elevated, supreme space of the cosmic computer does not register births on its home page. You have to become joy to be absorbed into it like oil poured into oil or water poured into water.

A winner become a role-model and provides (false) inspiration.

A loser becomes a coach or a therapist and

Provides (false) understanding and comfort.

A woman loves a winner and hates a loser unless the loser happens to be her own son or daughter.

A man is a sucker for a woman's beauty and therefore is forced to fight to become a winner.

Thus the process of pain and misery starts.

Take a deep inner look. The real inspiration is provided to us 14 to 18 times a minute through the breath which we breathe.

Be aware of the divine hidden in the breath and realize that the divine order is pre-ordained and pre-sent. Surrender to that order and undergo a transformation in your attitude and free yourself from doing.

Emptiness is not empty.

It is full of emptiness.

This fullness has a drug-like bliss.

Its overflow generates

bubbles of anti-matter.

This anti-matter is conscious.

Emptiness had awareness.

In particles of antimatter which is pure subjectivity, ego happens through a need to know what is anti-matter.

This need generates heat.

The heat crystallizes and solidifies, producing matter. The flow of energy from antimatter to matter is called kundalini or life force or anti-gravity.

This energy is conscious.

When it enters matter and takes possession of it, It becomes consciousness.

It is here that the opera of life happens and continues to happen till the material form of matter re-dissolves into anti-matter and consciousness becomes conscious, through anti-kundalini.

The field of anti-matter or pure subjectivity is unified and unilateral. You can say it is inter-netted.

Objective consciousness which means I, he, she, you or me appears to be separate and has separate portfolios.

But since the base is unified, it is safe to say that we are all children of the same subjective mother who clearly sees our objective differences and loves and cares for us accordingly.

But the father figure continues to be the full emptiness which is choice-less, passive but very full and very drunk with eternal spirit.

It is pure love without care. Anti-matter is love with care.

Matter is conditional love dependent upon its polarity opposite called conditional hate.

Conditional love is positive, conditional hate is negative. Love with care through subjectivity is neutral. And for pure love, no adequate word has been found so far because in that state there is no vocabulary.

It is pure being. Just being. Zero doing.

Enjoyable nothingness.

A spiritual holocaust.

Forever existing. Forever sparkling.

Pervasive without being invasive.

A perfect paradise, self-existing, self-evident, indestructible.

Not knowing anything.

Being nothing.

The source of all things. The master card. Absolute foolishness.

Forever masterly.

Words are inadequate to describe it.

Just "is" without need for any support. Eternally blissful. Eternally happy.

Eternally care-less.

I am that you are that Realize it.

The geo centre is absolute and therefore changeless. It is as it is.

The ego-centre or rather the ego-centricity is an equinoxal parallax caused by imagining to move that which is motionless and thereby creating a shifting declination, through a mathematical formula.

This shift causes shifting perceptions and helps the ego to experience mis-perceptions over the original perception.

Approximately 25000 years are needed for this shift to re-reach its original position.

This span represents ego-slabs like the Ice Age and the Stone Age.

Concentric circles around the ego-centre give birth to elapsed time theory.

What happens at the micro-level in one second may be experienced by macro-level after thousands of years and in slow motion.

The ego perceives. The master apperceives.

You are aware. It is only a statement.

It means nothing.

In order to experience awareness you have to become conscious.

Now, you are conscious. The first step has been taken.

It is called primary progression. It still means nothing and is very subjective.

In order to experience consciousness you have to identify yourself with an object.

Once that is done, you have successfully fooled yourself because now you are trapped in that object and are experiencing consciousness.

Without you, that object was lifeless.

The second step has been taken.

It is called secondary progression.

To unfool yourself, these two steps must be taken backwards.

The key to that is to be still.

Hence, the biblical statement "sit-still, realize the truth and free yourself".

It is that simple; but the fooled ego, loves complications.

So enjoy your complications.

The essence of the totality of all what is known to your subconscious is what you breathe in as your inspiration.

It inspires you to probe into the possibilities of the unknown which is limitless.

So no matter how much more of the unknown you discover, there will still be more to be discovered.

So you can never become the master of the unknown simply because it is limitless.

That leaves you with two choices.

Become the unknown or get out of the game of the known and the unknown.

Both really mean the same thing.

And then you will be a master.

You will be nothing and you will know nothing and nothing will bother you.

A master is never bothered for the same reason.

But where is the master? We don't see him because we are looking in what is known.

The master is not in the known.

Through self-appreciation, the need to be appreciated is destroyed.

Through self-fulfillment, the need to fulfill others is destroyed.

Through self-awareness, the need to experience consciousness is destroyed.

Contemplation destroys all needs.

Learning fattens all needs.

Learning is a mental process manufactured in the schools and universities.

Contemplation is an unbroken experience of the self in which the witness and the process and that what is witnessed appear as one.

So why can't we contemplate? Because of ignorance.

And what is ignorance? It is the mental process in which ratings, competitions, education are thrust upon us, forcing us to experience duality in an ever-widening gap.

Does the mental process have any reality? Investigate, and restore silence to the cosmic order.

Those who judge cannot be. Those who teach cannot do.

So it all boils down to being and doing.

True knowledge does not accept differences.

So being and doing have to be the same.

Perhaps doing is the reflection of being.

But for this reflection to become visible, there has to be a surface. Since knowledge does not accept differences, therefore it will not accept a surface.

So in the end it is only being. The doing, the reflection and the surface are all being.

Once you or I shall realize this, only then can we say that we know.

Till then we shall continue not to know and be victims of teaching and judgment.

See me as unreal and respond to my reality.

If you see me as real you will be disappointed, because I am virtual.

So in essence the game of life is to realize un-reality or rather to realize non-existence.

So why not just respond to each other and realize that our non-existence is already realized and stop wanting to make it more real and stop seeing each other as real.

Only then, can life be fun.

But our wrong seeing has trapped us into chains of illusions and no master is available to demonstrate how to correct our seeing.

There is no art in the heart. There is no science in the brain.

Art is a linguistic process.

Science is a numerical order.

Both are rooted in the intelligence of the ego.

Intelligence by its very nature is virtual.

All acts are acts of intelligence and therefore virtual. Sexing and thinking is all virtual.

Out of a false habit of seeing ourselves as real, we claim that sex and thinking are natural bio-psychic functions.

They are not. The naturalness of the unnatural cannot be stamped upon as natural.

Sex, thinking, acting, intelligence, can all be classified as mind.

Mind is an uncaused extroversion of the self.

Mind cannot exist without the self. Self can exist without the mind.

Be the self and free yourself from teaching and learning. Practice silence instead and restore joy within the self.

The seen universe is a mental digitality.

That what is, is merely a numerical order.

Its beauty lies in its alphabetic make-up.

Men are masters of numbers; beauty of the language belongs to a woman.

This is a very simple observation. Being numerical, nothing is impossible numerically.

Anything can be proved as true through numerical manipulation.

This would include numbers crossing swords with each other, through additions and subtractions and through square and cube roots.

In essence, numerically, the equation to prove god as a shepherd, or a carpenter or a teacher or whatever can be found.

What can't be proved is the opposite.

To say that something is not, implies crossing swords with zero (0).

The moment you do that, you cease to exist yourself because the zero would have reduced you to zero.

So you will not be able to know whether what you found out is true or not.

So says the wise one - first reduce yourself and then see if the universe is or is not.

And then you are free. Neither it is, nor it is not. Nor will you be; nor will you not be.

So the only sensible thing to attempt to win self-realisation is to cross swords with zero.

Anything multiplied with zero becomes zero.

The tarot calls zero the fool; the airy nothing, the unconcerned master; the only complete and powerful subjectivity with no beginning and end.

The most powerful tool of the magician; the master of illusions.

The chess comes very close in indicating the true nature of life. Let the king be silent and let the queen be aware. Let the king sit down peacefully and do his yoga. But the queen must have fun with her all-inclusive awareness. Remembrance that she must save the king at all costs never leaves her while she does her all-inclusive dance. So why is she doing yoga or allowing yoga to be pushed down her throat or becoming a yoga teacher? Is she bored with herself? Wake up women! The king is your un-born child. Entertain him with the beauty of your dance. Or do you want to have a boring un-born child. Do not fool yourself. You will never become the king. He does not exist. It is your imagination. Hey Mr un-born king. Wake up. What are you struggling and fighting for? Stop looking for your rights. You have none. She has them all. Sit peacefully and appreciate the beauty of her dance. Without your appreciation she will not feel like a queen. And that means the end of you. So be smart; do not interfere and allow her to improve the beauty of her dance through your appreciation. She cares for you. Do not seek confirmations from her. Or else, the dance will stop. And then you will never get born.

From emptiness to sound, from sound to light. From light to reflection.

From reflection to refraction. From refraction to quantum digitality.

From digitality to extension and duration.

And lo and behold, the universe appears in space-time. Suddenly I appear in it with ability to cognate and respond.

For my response to happen there must be a stimulus.

I fail to comprehend that the program to create external stimulus is pre-packed in my quantum back-pack.

And I go around claiming responsibility for my actions or am told to do so.

The joke is that I, who never was, now is and that who is now, never was.

What a stupid trap to be trapped in? I remember the words of my guru.

Do not be bothered he said.

You are not, so why should you bother.

Oh! My beloved guru, say that to me one more time.

The ego wants to beef it up.

The heart wants to milk it up.

Cow is the source of beef and best quality milk.

Its urine cures many biological disorders.

The dried cow-dung when mixed with wet mud makes a beautiful body pack which when applied and exposed to the sun cures many viral disorders.

A cow is a gentle animal which grazes on the joy of the grass-roots.

Therefore, the Hindus worshiped it as divine incarnate.

Restore dignity to the cow and the female divine

principal will regain its dignity forcing the male principal to do the same.

There will then be no need to hide or over-expose. Dignity neither over-exposes nor hides.

Joy will then become a natural divine order. So what are we waiting for? Some new God to beef us up?

The ego rises in the East and sinks in the West.

Astrologers call it the Ascendant –Descendant axis.

Emotion rises from the South and culminates as ambition in the North. Astrologers call it the MC-IC axis.

The interplay between ego and emotion gives rise to a cat-walk.

The astrologer calls it the nodal-axis or Rahu and Ketu. It is here on the cat-walk that behavior happens.

The only thing predictable about this behavior is its unpredictability.

Since the nodal-axis is illusive and uncaused, it has no real substance.

It is a technical illusion. Cat-walking primarily is a feminine principal.

The only function the male principal has on the cat walk is to be the ramp.

So the anatomy of an illusion is feminine.

The other is always the feminine. But the other is located in the brain and has therefore no locus standi.

Behavior, therefore is an illusion.

The only purpose it serves is to point out that the self too is unpredictable.

The only thing you can predict about the self is that it exists. Not as this or that.

In broader astrological spectrum, No.10 Downing Street has to co-exist with No.5 Upping Street.

Because this upping is natural and effortless, it is taken for granted.

It swings to No.10 before dropping down to No.4 of the astro heart.

This dropping should also be effortless at the culmination of ambition just like the ripe fruit falls down from the tree without any effort.

Because of ego, effort is made to hold on to No.10 position even after culmination.

There-in lies the humiliation and misery of the ego.

Other-wise, both up and down are natural to the self in its viewing of its appearance leaving it and returning back.

Some philosophers have hinted that the experienced universe is a mother's dream. Hence, parents playfully tell their infants "Aa-ja". Translated simply, it means come and go.

Insisting on transparency, while the need of the ego is to hold on to its apparency is absurd.

It will lead to chaos, confusion, mistrust and warfare.

It would be wiser to enjoy our apparency.

Joy is not volatile, does not lose its balance and has an all-round agreeability.

A day will come when our ego will get tired of enjoying the falseness of its apparency.

Only then will the real, transparent or rather the transcendental state of the supreme space of the self expose itself in the fullness of its sparkling glory.

Till then allow joy to be your best spontaneous habit and let it wear any habitat, it wishes to.

Till such time that we love our ego, which is the original sin, do not insist on the sin-less transparent state.

It will not happen as long as the ego is there.

Modern brain, specially the white man's brain has given a great gift to mankind.

The all famous inter-net which we are all enjoying.

For reasons best known to us, we fail to comprehend that we are already living in a network, the very logical astrological network.

Networking within a network is huge blunder. Consequently we shall all be thrown back to the East-point.

There we shall relearn to respect the cow and we shall be called cow-wards.

The internet is based upon man-made satellites.

Satellites are successfully created tumors in the cosmic body.

The chief destructive force of a tumor is its ability to create a rumour.

Rumour co-relates to the air element.

Living space is a natural amplifier.

Real and commercial winds will therefore begin to howl at unheard of speeds.

Emotions too, will do the same causing heart attacks to become as common as the common cold.

High time, we wake up and burn up these self-made tumors. Now.

Onslaught; aggression; need to impose generates excessive heat which is diabetic in nature.

Aridity happens as a consequence. We shall then be thrown to the mid-eastern point.

Sand will go into our hair and eyebrows. Then we will have to hate the pig.

It will look cleaner than us. Anguished, we will go down on our knees, put our heads down and beg for someone to insulate us till greenery or joy returns.

Or else; we will have to dig deep into ourselves and extract black oil from our bone marrow to survive.

This will crack our bones; just like the earth quakes when we keep pumping oil out of her structure.

And then even grass will refuse to grow. Joy would then be a far cry.

Earth will then become like Mars; a forsaken planet.

The East experimented with technology tens of thousands of years ago before finally abandoning it as unproductive.

Abandonment came automatically the day it respected the Cow; the divine mother.

Afraid that it might rebounce; the yogi finally, exported the number 0 (zero) to the Arabs; and freed himself from the futility of ball games.

Without zero; there is no technology.

The yogi faulted. Zero should have been dissolved and not exported.

So the zero (like all balls) has bounced back to sicken the Eastern mind again.

Now, it is the turn of the west to abandon it; which it will eventually.

Or else, the deluge. The re-start will be from the East. After setting; the sun always rises from the east.

Mother nature was at its very best in creating the Bermuda Triangle.

Bermuda Triangle was a brilliant, very practical un-thought thought.

Nature knows that a woman is not only attracted to power but has the ability to take it in and throw it out as an innocent joyful child.

Thousands of tornados and tropical storms pass along the corridor above which the Bermuda Triangle (a feminine principal) was located.

It used to suck in these tornados and throw them out as gentle drops of rain.

We probed and probed & have more or less destroyed the triangle.

Let's not run away from tornados. Give them a woman.

Create inverse triangles over their corridors, like mother nature did and free ourselves from the fear of their land-fall.

Let these tornados have some fun and not just enjoy the destruction they cause.

Let us stop thinking that we are cleverer than nature. Tirelessly, and thousands of times the guru said – observe, experience and enjoy.

Bring back that attitude and stop this modern habit – do no accept, challenge, analyze and conclude.

What a waste of precious time. Give space to the guru.

One word of wisdom from the mouth of the guru is worth more than the learning of a lifetime from these useless schools and useless universities.

They create intellect but destroy natural smartness.

They create a thought-process but destroy spontaneity.

They create excitement but destroy joy. And without joy, no game, including the game of life can be worth playing for.

So close these schools and close these universities.

It is the nature of the guru to be silent. Why? Because any spoken word can be faulted by changing the angle of its polarity.

If at all the guru had to speak, it was to the chosen one.

The chosen one trusted the guru and would not add or subtract to what he heard.

Hence the glorious "master-disciple" relationship.

The potency of the guru's silence had more sweetness than a million melodies.

Thousands gathered around the guru and heard his silence.

Some heard Om, others Aum, still others Ooom.

And the madness started. Is it Om, or Oom, or Aum or ching or chang? Ego never stops.

Frustrated, the guru left, sadness filling his heart. The egos could not even appreciate his silence without debating its context.

So we do not find the guru no-more. Silence your ego and he shall re-appear very happily as your own.photocopy from within.

So the guru is residing in your heart and only your silence will open the door of the heart.

No other master key will work, irrespective of how many techniques you learn.

Silence is not a technique. It is your natural state.

Chanting the name of the medicine a 1000 times is not going to cure the sickness.

Medicine must be taken.

Chanting that life is an illusion a million times is not going to get you out of the illusion.

That life is an illusion, is not a social chat or something to be debated about.

It has to be heard from the lips of a guru. Otherwise you shall not believe it.

How could you? You see pain, pleasure, torture, sufferings, everywhere.

How could this be an illusion? A guru is gentle but firm, loving and tolerant, unbiased, undifferentiated, not afraid, no matter what the circumstance.

Find such a person and hear from his lips that life is an illusion.

He will not find you. How could he? You do not exist in his vision.

Only then will you believe that life is an illusion.

The conviction of your belief will sink the illusion into your heart.

There, you will discover the virtual magnetic order of the mantra of the illusion.

Renounce the order and be free. Without that renunciation, the illusion will spring back into action at least 8.4 million times.

Such is its program.

What are you blaming the woman for? The ego is not a wave; the ego is not a length.

It is both. It is a wave length. The wave has its way.

It is wavy, and therefore called the queen's street.

The length is flat and boring. It is called the king's street.

The I-ching calls it the broken line and the straight line.

It is the wave aspect of the ego which has a double standard.

So double standard in not a western culture or an American syndrome.

It is just the way of the wave – an ascending octave and a descending octave.

This was very beautifully demonstrated by the actor-producer of Indian mythology called Shiva.

Shiva has two poses; the Nataraja or the dancing

Shiva and the meditative Shiva. In the dancing position

Shiva encourages his animus to be the whole universe or the master of the universe.

In his meditative position he discourages his animus so that the descending octave can have its dignity.

And not revenge itself back into action.

Hold on to your centre and enjoy your curves.

You will feel very beautiful, very dignified, very shy and very feminine.

Men will sit at your feet and enjoy the dignity of your beauty.

You will feel like a cosmic princess, very adored and least threatened.

Lose awareness of your centre and your curves will become very sexy, very exciting.

You will feel high but very threatened; both by male aggression and feminine bitchiness.

Your high will be short-lived; forcing you to become an angry and frustrated woman.

That signifies the end. Even god cannot save the universe when a woman is angry.

So please; let us see you as dignified and beautiful and not as sexy and exciting. Do not listen to me. Do as you feel.

I am only an opinion.

Hold on to your centre and enjoy your muscles.

You will feel very dignified, very calm and very composed.

Women will sit around you and adore you for held back position.

Flex your muscles and competition and aggression will begin, leading to war, misery, pain, humiliation with occasional jubilation of winning.

In the end, you will be destroyed. Someone will out-do you.

So please, be dignified, do not flex; and enjoy your calmness and restore peace to the cosmic order. But you do not have to listen to me.

Do as you please. I am only an opinion; albeit a sensible one.

When the fighting spirit of the "ram" loses and converts itself into "ashes", the guru and his "Ashram" happens.

Two kinds of gurus appear. The ego guru and the real guru.

The ego guru is a therapist or a coach who helps you to re-build your fighting spirit.

This is very foolish. The real guru assures you that no matter how big your fighting spirit is, you cannot conquer the spirit.

How could you? The fighting spirit has its source in the spirit itself.

So the real guru saves your ego from further humiliations and dissolves the fighting aspect of your ego back into its shape-less, formless self.

Cherish the real guru and keep a comfortable distance between yourself and the false guru.

Sven is mathematically a very clever name to give to the self.

Its inbuilt cleverness effortlessly generated its twin male and female aspects as SON and SKA. So Svenson and Svenska happened.

The female aspect found the male aspect very straight and very interfering.

So she encouraged Sven to become possessive about his son forcing him to add an extra S to Svenson to make it Svensson.

Sven's date warned him that this was a mistake which would become kali and very destructive after millions of years.

But he did it anyway. Because of this mistaken possessiveness, Sven become very egoistic. Ego is very vikingish in nature, so Sven became a viking and did his E-go.

His female aspect was very pleased because now she could just Go-Go, without constant irritation from her male counterpart.

So the phrase go-go girls is also a Swedish creation.

But now KALI has happened and Sven's 'data' has released a huge guilt syndrome into Sven as a karma punishment for that mistake.

This will force Sven to get to the rock-bottom of his cleverness to fix the mistake.

It is for this reason that many spiritualists including

His Holiness, the Dalai Lama have predicted that light will come from the North.

It has to because the darkness of the mistake originated from the North.

A guru giving diksha or instructions or the promise of enlightenment commercially or otherwise is more wrapped up in ego than you and me put together.

A real guru has no commercial centre, no commercial circumference and no hierarchy around.

His joyful silence will sink your ego into the real zero, the void, and not into the commercially computerized zero with its 64 connotations or enzymes, or hexagrams or archetypes or whatever you wish to call them.

The false zero is a stopgap; an infinity expander or a reducer.

The real zero is infinity itself. The self is beyond both these zeros. No name has been found for it thus far, simply because no one exists there to coin a name.

The two zeros are like tumors, one is malignant, the other benign. One gives pain, the other pleasure.

What a horrible pain? And what beautiful pleasure?

They have to have equal strength for the balance sheet of the cosmic ledger to be in balance.

Joy is the point of mutual negation of the duality.

It still is a concept. Religions call it god.

Here, absence and presence have no relevance.

It is also the launching pad of the ego. This is the last concept which the ego has to give up.

It is a sad occasion. It is the final farewell to arms, a point of no return.

And then the plunge. Memory and oblivion fade away; nothing remains.

All bonds are shattered, all charges dropped.

The chain of illusions snaps.

And you are what you have always been. Alone, permanent, blissful, unafraid, unconcerned.

So allow sadness to happen. It draws you closer to the final adieu.

Trust. Just trust. Not in God. Just trust. And the show is over. Instead, your completeness shines forever.

The day you are done with your E-go, the path to salvation will reveal itself.

If that day is today, ask yourself – Do I have desires? If the answer is yes, you are not ready.

Get up and chase your desires. If free from desires; hold on steadfastly to I AM.

Persistence in this will connect you to WE ARE. Individual mind will dissolve here.

You will feel elated. Effortlessly, WE ARE NOT will rise to negate WE ARE.

Tremendous joy will happen. Hold on to joy. A moment's blank and you shall drop into a well. All lights will come on. In this well of WE IS, there is abundant awareness of all kinds of beings.

From the lowly to the highest. Refrain from jumping into a being. A curtain will lift. Pure bliss will engulf you.

There you are helpless. Bliss takes over. It is the divine womb; your real home.

Whether this womb has its source in the lord itself is what I leave to your imagination.

What is comprised within you is not creation; but the creative principal.

It is common to all beings. Absolute spin and the absolute re-cycling of this creative principle generate its flow.

If you resist, you succeed in getting high-lighted; but the flow avoids you.

Release the resistance and it engulfs you; sending waves of rapturous joy through your very being.

The seen phenomenon is simply this highlighted resistance which we call creation.

But this creative principal has no prior knowledge of this creation; nor does its flow have any interest in this creation.

Therefore, it is said that God knows nothing. When all points of resistance dissolve; only joy remains.

It is at this point that the intellect faces a mental turmoil. If joy is all; then who was rotating and who was revolving? The intellect cannot find a solution.

The master steps in with the answer. It was a dream. The intellect accepts this; only after an intense exhausting struggle.

Memory then flies way. And what comes thereafter I do not know.

Simply because it cannot be known. Accepting this is realization.

Awareness of the creative principle reveals the obvious.

What is destined is not creation but the creative principle.

It will not change the logic of its course; no matter what.

In essence, it is very stubborn in following its path of least-resistance. Stubbornness belongs to a donkey.

A donkey and the ego therefore have a similar quality.

So this creative principle is not just the ego; but also its power-punch.

The individuality of this punch is numerically indexed in the stem of this creative principle.

The stem or the false "I" is the root cause of the creative principle and the creation it yields.

Uprooting this false "I" is accomplished silently by sitting in proximity of the Guru who is the ever-playful; ego-less child; with least interest in creation or volition.

It used to be said that if you do not know how to ride a horse; then you cannot ride a woman.

You tame a horse and you succeed in taming a woman. But a donkey is a different story.

The more load you dump on him the more stubborn he becomes.

To tame a donkey; let him be load-less. This is very beautifully picturised through card no 19 called Sun in the Major Arcana of the Tarot.

An innocent naked child is astride a donkey. The message is obvious. Effort fattens the ego.

Effortlessness destroys it. Then all your pasts, presents and futures are ready to be re-absorbed in the cosmic paradise.

Down with struggle; up through load-less-ness. Good heavens! It is the divine mother teaching us how to handle her.

Do you really need to be handled? Are you not fulfilled with the spirit of the lord? You confuse me, divine mother. I must be your dream. Please close your website.

Creation is as it is. Therefore, I am that I am. Your ego viewpoint observes and responds to this creation from the confines of this viewpoint.

So its response or its view is never wrong.

Put up a satellite and you become aware of response of other view-points and the war starts.

How could your view-point be wrong? It cannot be. Therefore the ego is never comfortable with losing.

A satellite is technology; the mother of mental sickness. Without the satellite there is no other.

You alone are. And you are the creation.

Temporarily, technology would be a day-dream. Eventually, it would be a nightmare.

Intuit the wisdom of this and say no to technology.

Now. Technology is the net-work of a sick mind. Sickness is much more complicated and exciting than health.

Eventually, it destroys health and you would not be able to enjoy the complications or excitements of sickness. Instead, it will enjoy you.

Going on-line to a perception is a technical impossibility.

On-lining a misperception is a contradiction; an error of judgment; or, an exercise in self-fooling.

The words of the master ring loud and clear.

"Nothing ever comes into existence; nor does anything cease to be".

The master can only indicate the paradox.

He cannot solve its riddle. How could he? It is beyond the intellect.

Intuitive understanding that I am seeking myself as the other, which is impossible has to replace intellectual hypocrisy.

Then life would be an experience of being lived; the actor-less acting.

Without that understanding, the paradox will haunt us.

We will fight; we will seek; we will destroy. Religion will dominate.

Power will dominate. Suffering will compound. Useless action plans will float.

The misperception will thrive till it sinks back into its source; which it will, no matter what.

Creation is a single act that never happened.

A visualized non-vision.

Accepting its own visibility as real, it transmutes, transforms, transmutates and translates into trillions of differences and trillions of universes.

The analogy is similar to a tree on a river-bank. While the tree holds on to its identity, its shadow ripples across the water creating differences.

The tree is helpless to stop its shadow from misbehaving and distorting its unity.

Similarly, the single creative act is unable to interfere in all the differences which appear merely in its presence.

So the wise one said "God never does anything.

His only contribution is his presence, without which the different universes are not". Read the first two lines again. They will clear your doubts.

Understand well the anatomy of an illusion.

The other is me expressed in reverse polarity.

Since the other invokes a response from me, therefore the illusion is referred to as feminine.

It does not mean a woman. It is within a woman.

The heart is always a woman.

There is "same-ness" in the heart. Sameness breeds familiarity.

Familiarity breeds contempt.

Contempt is the mother of the split.

The heart does not entertain this split and forces it to the brain at the speed of light.

This creates light-heartedness.

It also allows the heart to view its own split as entertainment.

Over a long, prolonged habit of viewing, this illusion has come of age and has achieved a "REALITY-STATUS".

And now the problem starts.

The illusion picks up ego and appears as "dry-wet" or "airy-fiery".

The airy-fiery is like a mirage which invokes thirst and inspires beauty and melody of the language.

The wet-dry is like a "visage" which appears as a "night-mare", quenches thirst, and creates a direct, un-mysterious language.

The neutrality of the split in the heart continues to be backstage and provides inspiration through a joyful and mythological kind of language.

Understanding this anatomy helps to reconvert

this uncaused illusion back into its basic function, an entertainment, the inner television, the inner play of maya.

The body is an electro-magnetic concept.

It does not say "I am the body or I experience pain". Now who is this "I" who is claiming responsibility? Investigate.

The word investigate is itself giving you a clue. IN-VEST-I-GATE.

So I enters and exits somewhere in the chest area.

The experience of the yogi is that this I when traced back seems to sink in the right side of his chest.

He calls it the spiritual or the ethereal heart. Ayurveda calls it OJAS-THAN. A minority in India (Sikhs) call their temple "Gurudwara".

Gur means Guru and Dwara means "through" or "gate".

"I" has a numerical value of 9 in numerology. 9th house is ruled by Jupiter in astrology. Jupiter is the guru in Hindu astrology.

The sign of the 9th house is Saggitarius which is written as an arrow (→) in western astrology.

Arrow points to the truth. Since this 9th sign is a part of whole circle of the Zodiac and can logically rise either from the 12th house or the 3rd.

I shall go no further with this. This indicates that all cultures had awareness of the origin of the conceptual universe.

This abstraction is a tribute to two mythological buddies SHIVA AND TOR and their very clever technician, Sven; and the ever playful son of Shiva named Ganesha.

The innocent idea for the universe came from Ganesha. Sven converted the idea into a concept.

Tor had his approval stamp (Tor's Hammer) and Shiva acted out the concept and played the universe.

Shiva and Tor had sambandh.

The word Sambandh appears both in Sanskrit and Swedish languages.

"Sama" means same in Swedish and "bandh" means bond or togetherness in Sanskrit.

So Shiva and Tor were bonded by the same code and Sven was the key.

Tamil was the ground language. "Ta" in Swedish means to take. "Mil" in the orient means to meet.

It was the fun of the 4th house – 10th house astrological axis.

Take a split at the end of the 4th house in opposite directions and reunite as sweet hearts at the end point of the 10th house.

This was the alter ego of the concept, its alternating current.

The straight flow from 4th to 10th was direct current of the concept.

So the network had 6 direct currents and 6 alternating currents eventually.

The blessings came from "SWAMI" the Tamil Guru.

"SOUMI LAND", the name of Finland has its roots in Tamil.

In fact Finnish language is very deeply rooted in Tamil.

Life is your wife. It cannot be your husband.

It gives you fun and pleasure as long as you are strong, healthy and beautiful.

It humiliates you and gives you misery when you are infirm and finally it leaves you. It uses you too, to keep her pro-creative act alive.

The church and the yogi saw through this.

Hence the emphasis on celibacy. The wise one first learns to live without a wife and then lives without a life.

What a glorious contradiction? Living without life.

But then the self is a contradiction.

Look at YIN-YANG. But in the eyes of the self there is no contradiction.

There is only the self. Oh! The frustration of this stupid duality.

Blind dates are unique.

There is so much excitement packed into them. Of course they may end up as total disappointments.

The moon takes 354 days to cover a lunar year.

A solar year has 365 days 6 hours. So 11 full days and one quarter day are blind dates.

Since they do not have the chance to be cooled down by the moon, they are full of energy and are born leaders. 11 of them are tall and one is short or a dwarf.

So the 12 signs of our zodiac were named after them, or rather they were the chosen leaders of the zodiac.

The shorter one, which only has 6 hours was given the privilege of being the chosen one and was given the 1st sign Aries or the "ram."

It was the divine woman's intuitive understanding that the shorter one had to be the more sensitive and therefore more egoistic and therefore more fun.

So it was her choice to let him have the privilege of ramming it in.

Since it would take 4 years to make the 6 hours into 24 hours (the leap year syndrome) therefore the chosen leaders normally run office for a 4 year term.

Of course the natural king of the Zodiac, "Leo", was angry.

It was his kingdom. Hence the constant war between the king and the leader.

The shorter sign or the dwarf is also called 'nata' in Hindi.

Hence the name "Nata-Raja" for Shiva which translates into short king and is therefore the woman's favorite and they worship its Lingam.

Incidentally most dictators are short people.

When a woman opens up, the man finds it very exciting.

When a man holds himself back, the woman finds it very exciting.

Such is the madness or the sadness of bi-polarity.

A sensitive man is in a horrible position. It is difficult for him to hold himself back.

Woman calls him cute but weak.

The Chinese call it broken yang.

It is very difficult for a cold woman to open up. So she is in a horrible position too.

Chinese call it broken ying.

A sensitive man would normally have an ill-placed Mars and a cold woman may have a badly placed Saturn.

It is for this reason that old astrology called these planets malignant.

All this is not a rule; just a general overview.

Understand the anatomy of a bio-chemical response.

When she sees a man her type, tremendous excitement is her first response.

Her stomach pounds with the stress of the excitement.

With great difficulty she pretends to be calm. Inwardly she hopes that the son of a gun will be man enough to take her right now.

When he sees her, his first response is appreciation of her beauty.

Her inner hidden excitement makes her more beautiful.

The moment she moves his appreciation converts into excitement.

So in a man excitement is a secondary response.

Immediately after the bi-sexual act, he becomes weak and beautiful.

She then appreciates his beauty. So in her, appreciation is a secondary response; excitement being the first one.

It is then that she gets angry. He is not beautiful enough.

She has more of it. Therefore, she has more chances of getting bored than he.

An extremely sensitive man is more beautiful than her.

Had he been taught to enjoy his sensitivity, he would become a master.

His first response would still be the same; appreciation of her beauty.

His secondary response would be to help her to become more beautiful, not through fulfillment but through joy.

She would call him a master all her life.

It is for this reason that masters were picked up by the Guru effortlessly when they were still kids.

A female master is exceedingly rare.

She has to pay the price for being a woman.

Her first reaction is excitement which is a loss of balance.

Masters do not get excited; neither as a primary response nor as a secondary response.

A master to excite a man is always a woman. Hence, the concept of cheerleaders.

Two waves make a length.

The length excites the waves.

And the waves recreate the length.

What a clever or horrible syndrome for the ego-virus to be trapped into.

So while we, as human virus continue to see our ego as pure and want to destroy other viruses, the anatomy of this syndrome will guide us into creating a sensible mouse-trap for the virus we wish to destroy.

It is called self-fooling. Create a self-spiralling wave length and float the virus on to it.

It will be trapped there till infinity unless it calms itself and purifies its soul, and is ready to be re-absorbed into the sea of spirituality.

There is an alternative to medicine.

Create a mantra-pill or a sound capsule.

"Aum" is the most potent mantra. When swallowed, this mantra-pill will create a counter spin to the viral spin of the virus.

The conflict between these two opposing spins will produce light. In that light, the ignorance of the virus will be destroyed and it will regain its spirituality.

I am suggesting "Sound" as an alternative medicine.

Before that, please close down these research labs and these researchers. Send them to piano schools instead, so that they can pick up the sensitivity to appreciate a sound.

What is this glory about the fortune of the three-legged-frog? It just helps you to jump into mental confusion.

Is the mind already not confused enough? Similarly, you cannot jump into now.

"Now" is not a time-mental state which is not there now and that you have to jump into it.

Why are we unable to recognize the "now" which always exists as now.

Simply because we are looking outwards. It is not out there.

Be old-fashioned.

Sit still and allow the 3-legged mental frog to withdraw back into the self so that the real "I" existence remains our permanent awareness as always "Now".

Not in now and here. Just "Now".

Understand well the anatomy of the mental attributes named need, greed and purity.

Need and greed are co-bonded.

Both are needy.

So they have similarities which are repulsive causing them to loath each other.

Purity is need-less, hence appropriate.

It is still a mental attribute which can be destroyed if we insist on a two-party system.

A single party system based on purity is impossible, since purity cannot stand-up to form a system.

A single party system therefore is a disguised need or a disguised greed.

So when purity comes your way, make the best use of it, by subsiding it, which would be very easy in the pure state. And then the mind will be killed and the glory of the self shall shine mindlessly, without the mentally attributed systems.

One memory of the flatness of his stomach, two reminders of his hairy chest and three drops of his huskiness when kept in a cognac glass makes a girl to have a glorious love high till the end of time.

Find such a man and freeze him into your memory bank and be fulfilled forever.

One flash of her lovely smile, two sparks of passion from her beautiful eyes and three drops of honey from her strawberry lips when kept in a champagne glass produce a love-high till the end of time. Find such a girl and freeze her into your memory bank and allow her to hypnotize you till the end of time.

When these two memory banks stare at each other and succeed in doing so forever, it is called scientology - a unit of science.

If they succeed in creating oneness forever, it is called spiritology a unit of the spirit.

Those who are incapable will not be disappointed. The cosmic computer offers an alternative.

It is called mythology – unit of myth.

So all can have fun. Don't blame God. The cosmic computer is perfect. Use it smartly. You are God.

Acupuncture is retarded. It is invasive. Acupressure is a lot smarter but unnecessary.

Its operating principal is to press out the pain through gentle pressure.

Internal acupressure exists too. The yogi gave it to us as "PRANA-YAMA", the breathing yoga.

Modern medicine is the biggest modern blunder. It is more stupid than a donkey.

Herbiology is a lot smarter. The yogi gave it to us as ayurved.

Ayurveda has left behind the legacy of herbiology. Awareness of the breath and spotting of the divine order hidden in the breath unlocks many of the diseases of the mind caused through need and greed.

The sound of the divine order is very similar to the deep resonance of the church bell.

If you hear it in the breath, you will be sitting in the peacefulness of the church without being in the church.

So, sound cures the mind and light cures the body.

Why do we run to the doctors and their power? It is the fear of pain, fear of dying, fear of losing our loved ones and the fear of losing our beloved body.

All these are habits. Body is the first biological habit. Experience is the first psychological habit.

Food and water too are elementary habits. The breath contains the essence of food and water to sustain the body.

How do we overcome these habits? By realizing that they are not the way to eternal happiness.

Experience must stop. The only experience should be the experience itself.

Not the experience of this and that. Your sensitivity will enable you to intuit the truth of what I am saying.

That sensitivity itself becomes the biggest obstacle.

Seek a guru who straightens out the act of sensitivity. In essence, the female principal must reabsorb into the male principal and unity is thereby established.

Modern shrinks are masters of gray zones.

How could they not be? They cause them. Or rather their need to fix them keeps the grey zones alive.

Suggest this to them and they will explode with anger exposing the truth of their inner imbalance.

We put them on chairs. High chairs. They hang their diplomas behind their chairs.

The real chair belongs to a master. Master's only strength is his inner silence, through which he enjoys your being, causing you to reconnect with your inner mainstream effortlessly.

Extra sessions are not necessary. No price is paid. No price is expected. The master is a rare one.

Shrinks are too many; their noise too loud; their cleverness overly misguided.

They destroy potential masters to keep their chair alive. Sadly, they know the dirtiness of their inner truth but keep going anyway.

Uprooting traumas or correcting the stances is a modern mental blunder, its temporary relief baits us into a sense of wellbeing but its after effects damage the psyche more.

Uproot by all means. But uproot the psyche or rather the ego itself and not the traumas which are countless through countless lives.

It would take eons of light years to uproot all the traumas one by one.

Latitudinal corrections anger the bio-spin. Longitudinal interferences cause severe mental oscillations.

The core of ancient wisdom highlights the fact that spiritual life force and water have a similar logic. Leave it alone and it re-finds its level effortlessly.

Let it enjoy its level without attitudinal judgments and it becomes like a peaceful lake enjoying its ripples endlessly.

Apply this logic to all your plans of global warming, ecological corrections or saving the planet.

No action plans will come forth. There will be no Nobel prizes; no TV coverage. Instead, we will enjoy our level and all will end well. Joy cannot impose.

It is not in its nature. Self is joy. Joy is self. Self exposes without any mental need to prove the exposition.

How can it? Mind is the exposition. How can an exposure suffer? It is a contradiction.

So who is the sufferer? Find the answer. There is only suffering but no sufferer.

When suffering and sufferer are one, then only bliss is the experience.

"Non-existence", thy name is a woman. The most beautiful ever.

"Existence" is her unborn baby. All the unborn potentials of existence are competing to be the chosen one. All this is that.

One of us will be chosen. It is a "21 days" contest. 18 days are spent in fighting and competition.

Then the chosen one enters her foetus to be the next "star" to be born.

The one who is least bothered is her favourite. So stop bothering.

But remember, her name is "non-existence", her nature is existence.

Non-existence cannot give birth to existence. So all this is her dream.

But do not blame her. Dreams happen by themselves. So she is not a mean woman. She is the most beautiful ever.

She is the only "existence" which appears on her screen of "non-existence".

These "18 days" are stretched out as one phase spawning 4.32 million years.

Her flexibility has the sensitivity to spin time waves. Adore her, worship her and realize your nature which is a woman.

And then the miracle will happen. You will realize that "non-existence" is the nature of knowledge.

And "existence" is the dreamed out nature of "non-existence".

Where do we fit in all this? Well, figure it out. We don't.

Heart is bi-mental. The brain is tri-mental. The boss is unimental.

This can be re-phrased. The boss has unilogy, the heart has bio-logy and the brain has tri-ology.

The boss is God. So that leaves us a heart with two-wheels and a brain with three wheels to play with.

Men love bi-cycles and children play with tri-cycles. That leaves a woman with no rights.

Men love that concept. But ask a woman.

She knows her truth. She has no interest in your bicycles and tri-cycles.

She just loves those fast, slick 4 wheeled with a lot of horse power. So in the end, it is a woman's universe.

She controls the four elements of universe and gives birth to bicycles and tricycles.

To understand confusion, the Chinese philosopher took the name of Confucius.

He sat glued to "I-ching", the book of change where the code of confusion stood like a nightmare.

In the end Confucius got very confused thinking why confusion was so confusing.

Buddha finally hit the nail on the head.

He allowed himself to drown in that confusion without struggle.

Confusion turned out to be his friend.

It drowned Buddha's ego completely and re-surfaced him without his ego.

Buddha re-birthed into a super star.

The story of Nanak has a similar history.

So embrace your confusion and stay away from behaviour specialists who are masters of milking your confusion.

That is their skill.

A bit more on the catwalk.

The Hindus called it the Karma axis. Some others call it the axis of evil.

Attempts have even been made to veil it. It is uncaused. As long as the moon revolves around the Earth the catwalk will happen.

Mythology calls it the damsel who fooled the Gods. Chinese call it the dragon.

No matter what, it has established its permanence on the astrological web-site.

It is snake-like and therefore a trend-setter. It puts on the make-up of the opposing signs it falls on.

One is a credit the other a debit, a pleasure or a pain.

Its axis excites economic trends too since it can fall across the face of a low tide or high tide moon.

Mayan Indians predict a shower of black snakes.

Manmade satellites which will also produce nodal axis is the thesis of that prediction.

The intellectual philosopher glued himself to the "Orange-order" of the confusion.

The yogi demonstrated the order through his Achtanga Yoga.

The woman danced out the Tao of the confusion.

Because of their fascination with the order, they got more attached to it. It got them nowhere.

The Guru ignored the order, gave it no importance and the ego of the order fled, the Guru won his freedom.

He attained his Samadhi. And flew off into the heavens. Beyond all beyonds and attained the very rarely attained Siva-loka, the state of the self.

Through intense one-pointed concentration an elemental order crystallized and took on the format of an orange hue.

The zealous missionary marched out the orange order.

The airy-intellectualist chartered the hexagrams of behaviour while scrutinizing the order.

The fiery yogi did the achtanga of the order. The watery artist composed his music watching the flow of the order.

The beautiful woman exuding confidence over her beauty tried to seduce the order.

Infuriated, the order hit back causing her to bleed. She bleeds to-date everytime the order comes into its cyclic phase of a bad mood.

The guru embraced the order.

And the ego of the order fled, causing a complete dissolution of his body without dissolving his awareness.

So all we have to do is to detach ourselves from the hypnosis of this order and enjoy its mischievousness like a child cnjoys a toy.

Essence of religion is to help us to break this order-habit through de-concentration.

How then have we succeeded in making religion such a serious business? Seriousness is concentration, the source of misery.

So understand well that the anatomy of religion is playfulness devoid of the concentrated need to win or to impose, to punish or to retribute.

All these are constituted in the order, attachment to which is what religion tries to break through spiritual awareness.

The float-valve is in the heart.

The "think-tank" is in the brain. Purities are kept in the heart where Lady Venus enjoys a luxurious bath.

Impurities are sent to the brain to be "thought-out" and "fought-out".

The rectum and the urinary tract throw out the gross garbage.

The brain gets rid of the subtle garbage.

The heart folks have the joy of inner luxury written all across their face. Brain folks pretend to be happy.

Saturn, Rahu & Ketu are the servants in the brain.

Moon supervises them. To dignify themselves, they call themselves public servants.

Out of their pretended dignity they create a spectrum of outer luxuries, but remain dirty inside.

The ground floor folks have a gross cleaning job to do.

They are obvious and cannot hide their frustration.

The sound of the mantra of the lower Chakra is "Bhang". Therefore these people are called Bhangis or Sweepers.

Their job is physically exhausting.

They make up for it by drinking Bhang, a country made liquor. Mars is their supervisor.

Tantra has given all the keys. Search it more deeply.

In the end, it is the woman, who stands to scrutiny.

Why? I do not know. As the saying goes, "Alone, the eagle must fly across the face of the sun".

I have been fascinated by the beauty of women.

But sadly enough, there is only the 'Mother-child' relationship which is "Nickel-free".

Therefore a woman is chosen to give birth to a child.

Birth through desire is contaminated. A desire-free sexual act is a contradiction.

Hence desire creates the universe and its absence negates it.

Who is to blame? The culprit is the inability to tolerate one's own presence which causes the original split. And the fighting starts.

The split takes over. What a fascinating split? It is the lunar axis. It is as it is. It does not see the split. How can it? It is nickel-free.

Intellectual spirituality has no potency.

How could it? The inner division of the mind itself robs you of your spiritual value; leaving you with very little net worthiness.

Without net worth, the network of the feminine divine principle will be inaccessible.

It does not allow you entry. The cleverness of an Einstein is not needed to realize that the female essence is the network which baits the masculine principal through its inherent quality of make-up.

Before the battle of the sexes begins, it would be wiser to contemplate that both male and female energies are feminine with alternating polarities.

Therefore the universe is a woman's dream. When she wakes up; there is no more universe or its values which we cherish so dearly.

Wait for her to wake-up. You are her.

Why acupuncture the body, when the Ace is up your sleeve.

It can be directly activated.

Why look inside the body with lasers and x-rays when the information is on your fingertips.

Re-establishing joy only takes 14 days of awareness.

It is the highest education.

Other educations that take more than 14 days to learn are counterproductive and toxic.

It will contribute to misery and not to joy. Joy is our natural state.

It takes 14 days to blossom and 14 days to un-blossom into a new round of joy.

Continued awareness of nature is the key. Learning is a classroom mistake. A control trap.

Sven of Sweden made Vodka to keep his head warm.

Gupta of India made yoghurt lassi to keep his head cool. A whisper floated across their horizon.

"I am modern MBA. I shall teach you my tricks.

Come drink my summer wine over a 3-year period and I shall reward you with a diploma".

Both went. Brilliant methods to manipulate the trade-winds and to milk the co-lateral's confusion were taught under the guise of business management.

Armed with their business diplomas Sven and Gupta returned home; much sharpened in their cleverness but much blunted in their wisdom.

Shortly thereafter, the madness started. Sven now wants to sell Vodka to Gupta to heat up his already hot head.

Gupta wants to market lassi to Sven to chill his already cold head.

This is not freedom of the market. This is incorporated stupidity "A La Harvard".

The cover-up too is brilliant. Hey, you don't have to buy; I am only suggesting but not forcing.

Conceptual self-ignorance is pancreatic and kidnetic in nature.

Over-sternness and over-kindness dries it out.

The one who sings is called a singer, the one who does is called a do-er and the one who lives is called a liver.

Obviously, your ego self-awareness is trapped in your liver.

Arrogance heats it up; remembrance of the lord calms it.

Calmness is your best way out. Your carbon emission is what you breathe in as your karma retribute.

The day your out-breath is carbon free, the real awareness will gladly embrace you.

The seen universe is your carbon print-out.

A cow has been gifted to you. Every part of it, except its meat is pure. Drink its milk.

Watch its bliss and purify your soul. We are a computer virus.

Mamma earth is a specially created website for us to fulfill our virus-itic needs.

Advanced computer systems will also have an in-built virus web-site as a security precaution.

Any time a virus happens, deliberate or un-caused, it will find its way to this web-site immediately.

Bogus information will be stored in this web-site for it to feed its lust upon.

Some religions have the master-key to attack real websites too.

This will infuriate the lord. The computer and its virus share the same intelligence.

We can frustrate the lord; but we cannot affect it directly.
Religion proclaims that we are here to purify our soul.

So, obviously, we must be an impurity. Accepting that will purify us.

Your body needs the food which grows in your country. Your mind needs the language of your country.

Your soul needs the culture of your country. Do not be fooled by the neighbour's grass.

It always appears greener.

Human race is very fond of experimentation. I suggest an experiment too.

Make falling sick a punishable crime unless the sickness happens to be a common cold or a viral disorder or hereditary or accidental.

Results are almost predictable. Health will improve. Earth will dance with joy.

There will be no heart attacks or earthquakes.

The animals will regain their playfulness.

Human beings will experience renewed joy.

Doctors will feel very sad. Pharmaceuticals will have a long face.

But before the experiment happens, the intellectual mafia will debate me out.

The writing is clear on the wall of the third eye. Anarchy cannot deliver.

Hierarchy is inadequate. Monarchy has to be the answer.

Bring it back. Monarchy is in your heart. Anarchy is mental mafia. Hierarchy is physical mafia.

The corrupt Hindus amass wealth.

To overcome their guilt, they donate a small temple. The Americans do the same.

They create a mental top thrcugh their White House and overcome their guilt by playing baseball, a ground floor game.

Cultures originate on their latitude.

Its mental state is its longitude. Both are determined at birth.

Religion could therefore be called the longitude of the latitude.

Spirituality lies in our attitude. That is our only freedom.

Longitudes converge in bi-polar regions to create mental or physical orgasms. A master is a spiritualist, an attitudinist.

His wisdom is contained in the words "Be as you are". It automatically allows the other to be what they are.

With this attitude, violence, bias, competition, anger have no existence.

This pleases the boss of the cosmos and paradise happens on earth.

If not, we are not very far from living hell.

Hear the right words. Not from me. But from the master and win paradise.

Our gratitude to the Holy Father or for that matter to the Holy Mother for holding themselves back.

The power of their celibacy allows us to have fun. Hold yourself back through effort and you shall be in a painful holy state.

The universe shall then be in your composite opposite, the state of forced pleasure.

But this is not pure; since holding back was through effort.

The moment the effort will become stronger than you, you shall spring back into the unholy turmoil.

Hindus call the state of being held back without effort the permanent bliss of samadhi.

It happens when you are blind to the universe. It is not seen.

How can it attract you when not seen? So be blind. Be in love. Love is therefore said to be blind. Unconditional.

Women of today are stressed. White or blue collared jobs produce stress.

Stress makes a woman less pretty. That is sad. But stress can be straightened out.

So women need to get smarter. Here are some pointers:

1. Remember that what is good for the goose is not good for the gander.
2. "Management" is for men. Insist on education and diplomas on "womanagement".
3. Stressed men de-stress in bars. They are called pubs. The theme of the pub is "we drink to wives and sweethearts, may they never meet'. A woman's bar is called a hub. Dance out your stress in the hub with the theme "we dance to husbands and lovers, may they never meet."
4. Your children need the love of their father, not of your lover.
5. Do not fall in love with your lover. Use him as a mister. His only job is to bang the hell out of you. Buy him gifts.
6. Have intellectual male friends. Allow them to hold your hand and an occasional kiss. Respect them. Golden words of wisdom shall come out of their lips.
7. Discuss lovers with no one.
8. If a man lover is in-adequate, do not indicate your disappointment to him. Tell him he is too beautiful and that you are afraid to fall in love
9. with him and split. Do not hurt him. Playful lying is necessary. It is not a sin.

10. Be a woman. Do not copy a man.
11. Start to see through sex. It is the original sin.
12. Buy more make-up. It is your best cover-up.
13. Through post-graduate education in womanagement train female masters to teach house-husbands how to put their heart in cooking and laundering.
14. Encourage house-husbands to sing and dance. It is healthy for the kids.
15. Allow your house-husband to polish your toenails while you are busy doing your morning make-up.
16. Listen to your house-husband. He is your wife after all.
17. Refrain from stealing each other's husbands. Impose strict harshness for committing this unholy sin. This will protect family hierarchy.
18. Interest of children comes first always and every time.
19. Do not scream at your house-husband in front of the kids. They will start to feel sorry for him. Unhealthy.

A few tips for all of us:

- Stop begging from God. He has nothing to give. Not to beggars anyway.
- Words will never reach God. Your silence has a better chance.
- Stop trying to be positive. It will only produce negativity. Read a funny book instead.
- Stop your need to give. Giving is not a need.
- Trying to love thy neighbour as thyself without you being in balance is like asking a fish to walk. Be in balance. Correct behaviour will follow by itself.
- Fulfill yourself before you fulfill others. But, remember that emptiness is the best fulfillment. It is full of emptiness.
- Your heart will show what you have. Your brain will focus on what you do not have. Go beyond have and have not. That is where God lives.
- Love if you will. Be angry if you will. But do it well. God loves good performances.

Why is it said that it is a man's universe?

Look at the dollar sign. Interaction between two sticks produces a wave. Masculine energy. Erect a dollar sign and see it in its plan view. It will look like Ying-Yang. If ying-yang is seen as a unit of money and folded inwards along its central wave so that the ying is on one side and the yang on the other (like all units of money) it will look like a mango on rather "man-go"; masculine energy. Ying-yang has 64 coins. The old Indian Rupiah had 64 paisas. Rupiah in the orient means that which gives shape and form. 64 is the first available number which contains both space and time components. $4^3 = 64$; $8^2 = 64$. 100 cents of a dollar only has time; $10^2 = 100$. In order for it to have space it should have 1000 cents. So in the decimal system time is separated from space. Space is kept at the background so that male time can happen. Unless the idea is to make a "times square"; $8^2 + 6^2 = 100$. But then the twin towers will have an unequal height or base plan. If these two towers are seen as man and woman, then the woman: man ratio would be 3^6:64. But since it is a man's universe based upon male energy, both men and women are conceptually female with different make-ups. The real woman lies hidden behind in her divine form (Maya-Devi). Therefore the source of the mind (in which man and woman appear separate) and the inspiration they need has to lie in the fertility of this divinity who borrows her energy from the un-seeable, un-fathomable self. This self continues to be the only witness to this spectacle which is neither attached to it, nor separated from it: but cannot appear without it.

Collective emotional attribution is un-emotionally retributed by the divine to restore the status quo. The divine itself being motion-less is not attached to this retribution or to its consequences. So it cannot laugh or cry over it. This interference of the divine is called a backlash or absolute reversal. This backlash is a logical, collective unemotional response to collective emotional doing. Some religions have established this as God's will. The entire structure of this religious approach is based upon the tit for tat principle and backlashing is technically applied. The Tarot calls this card Justice, marked 11 in its major arcana. This is digitally very sound. Every act has a numerical strength. When any whole number is reversed in its polarity, it is automatically divisible by 11. So, eleven shows up as the control number. Number 11 indicates two creative acts comprising a forward slash and a back-lash. But numbers are mental. So this divine act is also mental, and when looked for, neither the acting principle nor the reacting principle would be found. Mental divinity is no divinity at all. So the entire working principle of the universe is a mental concept which cannot stand-up on its own; hence un-real. While we are in this un-reality, it will not give space to question its un-reality or reality.

Life is a game. Planning and thinking out your composition (Ishtam) to go on-line at the appropriate time (Lagnam) is a pre-game function. While in the game, there are two choices. One choice enables you to observe and respond. To co-ordinate this function, the two co-ordinaries Ida and Pingala have been given to you. They are self-adjusting. Through learning of yogic "Prana-yama", they can be manipulated. The joy of observing and responding is ordinary since it is dependant upon the two co-ordinaries. The French call this "Vin ordinaire". The second choice is contemplation. In this choice Ida and Pingala lose their significance and you begin to evolve. The index of your evolution is registered in the central shaft called Sushmana. Americans call it the Wall Street. This too can be manipulated through yogic exercises or through mental trickery taught in the business schools. The joy is greater in contemplation than in observation. The French call it the "vin superior". Sushmana touches the 3rd eye before curving back to the ethereal heart where a red-carpet applause awaits it. Here, double or quits is offered to the ego. The manipulators who aroused Sushmana through yoga or business schools are severely reprimanded and ordered to repeat the same program.

The relationship that Siva has to Shiva is the same relationship which self has to a shelf. The difference in these two states lies in the alphabet "H" whose numerical value is 8. 8 when squared produces 64 intonations or functional enzymes in the human body. So in essence, there is a totality or a warehouse from which one "ware" is downloaded to experience "a-ware-ness". This totality is a programmed senselessness. This senselessness is aware. Just aware. Not aware of any particularity. The programme of this downloaded "ware" is virtualized by the help of the five senses which represent the first five chakras. Since this programme is a downloaded experience of a fraction of the whole, therefore it is called an illusion.

The anatomy of the flow system of these illusory five . senses is as under:

IS IS　　　　IS IS NOT

↑

IS

↑

I AM IT

↑

IT IS

↑

I AM

Space –time has its own operating principal which is as under:

$SHE^2 + HE^2 =$ TIME. Root Cause Existence

$SHE^2 + HE^2 =$ SPACE. Root Cause Matter

Sixth sense is the boss. It is the brain and it can rule through an iron hand or a kid glove. Senselessness is in the ethereal heart. All this sensory experience is the sweetheart of the nameless self which never leaves the self. When this sweetheart aspect within the self is experienced as the self, it no longer is an illusion but an unbroken, eternal experience of the self without any subject -object relationships. To get there is the aim of all spirituality.

Black is beautiful. So is white. Take a paint box. Mix black and white colours together. It yields gray. Gray is a very powerful natural depressant. So it is not a very healthy mix. This is very simple observation; not mental in nature. Symbolism of ying-yang highlights this observation directly. Biological; not mental apartheid between black and white is therefore sensible. Chinese knew it. Therefore ying-yang. Apply your mind to it and it becomes racism. We do not mix things that do not blend well except as medicine. Is it a racial issue? Mind of course can find faults with anything. It could argue that the sperm is always white. So is truth. But then are all white people truthful? Graduate from black to white or from white to black through brown. This is wisdom not racism.

We all know where the circular top White House is. It is on the top of a woman's head and at the end of a man's dick. What are women doing out there. It is not their domain. We also know where the dark, artificially lit, triangulated roof top church is. It is in-between a woman's legs and at the top of a man's head. So what are men doing in the church? It is not their domain. The job of the dark hole is to convert the white aggression into joy. So women should be teaching us celibacy and not create a need to excite aggression; just so to convert it into joy. But if it happens; let a child be born. If we close the black hole what will the white house do with its power? It will no longer be aware of it. So says the spiritualist –"in its pristine state, the self is not aware of its awareness. It just is".

Take an unbiased look. The top of the White House is very male. The top of a Church is very female. Equal blend of these two principals is what a temple top looks like. Neither too round, nor too triangulated, but in the middle. Every-one there can be accommodated in the temple to celebrate joy. But the White House is for men and the church for women. This is how the three principals of the mind behave. Positive, negative or neutral. So, why the controversy? Whatever comes your way becomes your way.

A guru will not understand you. What use will that false power have? A Guru will not over-stand you. Why should he impose his will upon you? Instead, he uses his flexibility to come to your level to connect you to your being. That is his grace. Imitating role models who are way beyond you will only give you a temporary kick-start. Eventually, it will frustrate you, depress you and make you feel like a loser. His role model is He + 1. Continue on this ladder till you reach your optimum level — the Absolute Beast. Her role model is SHE – 1. Continue on this ladder till you reach your optimum level — the Absolute Beauty. At the optimum levels, the polarity reverses to re-reach the original position. Without this reversal, the HE/SHE unit will not have self-generating power. What a clever or a horrible syndrome for the HE/SHE virus to be trapped into!

Are we outcasts? Are we un-wanted? Are we really here? Or, have we been sentenced to life? Deeper contemplation may dissolve this mystery.

Have you ever heard of anyone asking for lefts? No. We want to know what our rights are. Left therefore is subjective, taken for granted, depended upon. It is not a woman. It is God.

Left is. Right acts. All actions are therefore right. An action can not be wrong because it is spontaneous and left supported. So why do we punish people for actions? What prompts us to judge them as wrong? It is the brain. All actions which are brain-planned are wrong actions. Life is a game. We are in it.

Planning is a pre-game function. So stop planning. Play life. Let your left support you.

No action would then be a wrong action. It would always be a "now" action. This present madness of making action plans must end. Stop chairing committees. Do not impose yourself or your intelligence on the left.

It is smarter than you. Stop this crime and punishment. A few tough years will have to be paid as retribution price for all these rights and wrongs committees we have created. Stop inventing. Enjoy what has been created naturally. Allow one generation of children to have fun. Stop sending them to these useless brain-schools and brain-universities.

A seven-year price as investment in joy of children will transform the world into a joyful place.

Your action plans will damage joy. Allow the political and religious hierarchies to crumble like a house of cards. In spite of all this, our positive "doings" or our negative "non-doings" are not going to affect the one which is beyond all doings. So in the final analysis, nothing matters.

How could a photocopy's doings or non-doings affect the "wholeness" of the original?